I0181678

HOLY
TERROR

In The Name of

The Father

The Son and

The Watchtower

Ritchie Mac

HOLY TERROR

In the Name of the Father, the Son, and the Watchtower
Copyright © 2014 by Ritchie Mac.

All rights reserved. Printed in the United States of America. No part of this book may be used or reproduced in any manner whatsoever without written permission except in the case of brief quotations embodied in critical articles or reviews.

This book is a work of non-fiction. However, names, characters, businesses, organizations, places, events and incidents either are the product of the author's imagination or are used fictitiously. Any resemblance to actual persons, living or dead, events, or locales is entirely coincidental.

For information contact: info@uptownmediaventures.com

Book and Cover design by:

Freedom Underground Publishing,

(a completely independent imprint of Uptown Media Joint Ventures)

ISBN: 978-1-68121-001-8

First Edition: January 2015

10 9 8 7 6 5 4 3 2 1

This book is dedicated to those who remain silent out of the fear that has crippled their minds and hearts, in order that they MIGHT live forever. This book is also dedicated to my father who I love so dearly but never really had the chance to show him completely. I hope this book will make you proud dad.

Chapters   **Pages**

Introduction

I remember the times when my own silent thoughts would send me into panic attacks because I really believed that Satan was with me. Certainly a servant of the only true god Jehovah would know that literally everything that is spoken or written from god's "only" spirit directed organization is "The Truth". To question or worse yet to doubt anything that comes from the Watchtower society is proof in itself that Satan has influenced the mind and essentially forfeited all hope of a promise of eternal life after Armageddon.

I noticed at a very young age that most of the congregation members seemed to have some sort of mental health issue(s). Of course I wasn't aware of the term mental health as a child but I clearly understood the characteristics of a person who was anxious, hurting and fearful of everything in everyday life. I more often than not, overheard my mother talking to her friends about all the things that others in the congregation were doing and how they knew these people would lose their lives in Armageddon. This was illustrated very graphically in the *My Book of Bible Stories* which took fear to an all-time new height, hence the title of this book.

From the threat of imminent death if I wasn't perfect in the eyes of the Watchtower society, to being verbally molested for confessing my sin, to public humiliation of being read off as publicly reproved which instantly branded me as being bad association, to losing my father in almost every way because he was disfellowshipped, my life as a Jehovah's Witness was Holy Torture.

Chapter 1

Holy Torture

It would be my mother who would be the final reason for me to decide that it was time to put my religiously ingrained fears aside and start to research my pseudo faith. I say pseudo because I would later realize that my faith rested with the promises of men and not god (this is not a typo) who I still have not yet come to truly know or understand.

Anyway, my mother scolded me for being in association, on public media, with a young woman my age who we considered to be family. The passing of this young woman's mother has scarred my mother because they were inseparable. This is why I was actually disgusted that my mom became upset with me because this young woman wasn't attending the meetings at the Kingdom Hall anymore yet she was one of the most well-grounded individuals that I knew. I'd like to thank my mother for aiding me by her own words and actions, to a path of true deliverance out of the Watchtower organization.

I knew that, by researching the origin and background of the organization, I was setting myself up to lose all the people that I had come to truly love. That didn't bother me as much as my greatest fear - that my then 16 year old daughter would shun me in her heart. She understood very well that those actions were not permitted. I had raised her to believe what I was taught. There is no other true religion but the Jehovah's Witnesses.

I remember that I prayed sincerely. I did not address my creator as Jehovah God. I addressed him as Father. I actually had a conversation with him although I wasn't certain that my prayers were even being received. I reasoned to myself that as long as I keep my prayer respectful I should be able to tell my Creator exactly how I felt and the effects that those negative thoughts had on me.

I told my creator, my Father, that I hated the Kingdom Hall. I hated reading the Bible too. It taught me nothing but more fear and confusion for Him and for life. I told my Creator that I'd rather die knowing that I sincerely tried to search for Him than to live now in total resentment of Him and His "so-called" organization and to blindly follow the life "they" chose for me, only to end up dead in the end anyway. That prayer was the beginning of freedom and after saying "amen" I felt good. I was ready. Set. Gone!

No more two and three hour long meetings, three days a week, to listen to hypocrites tell me how to live my life. No more fashion shows to see who appeared to have the richest parents by way of their own dress code. Gone were the days of having to turn my head during a whole ride home during the Christmas holiday season because we were not allowed to find beauty and amazement in anything from Satan. Those darn lights were used as weapons to temp our little unsuspecting hearts into wanting the glamorous things that Christmas and Satan's world seems to boast.

One of the greatest feelings came from knowing that no more pioneers and elders would be knocking on my door unexpectedly because I missed a meeting or two. I'd never have to knock on another stranger's door and pass over education that could pay for my living expenses, in order to serve as a full time pioneer (evangelist) in the name of the organization. I wouldn't have to turn in my strictly monitored ministry hours anymore to prove my love and dedication to god. The list is endless but I will attempt to uncover these things as I take you through my life of a very literal holy torture.

Chapter 2

Taking My Stand

Every year in school, around the holidays, there would be some sort of party thrown at school. These parties were always overflowing with lots of candies, cakes, chips and anything else that would make a kid happy and possibly hyper!

As the food and sometimes gifts were being set upon my desk I would be making my exit out of the room to go to the library to join the other Witness and a few Muslim kids. It was amazing how we all spoke with pride but almost in a perfectly rehearsed tone. We smiled and colored or watched movies as if we were the happiest kids around. Sometimes the librarian would give us snacks probably in an effort to alleviate our true sadness of being left out.

When I would return to the class I always felt different. Of course that's the way we were trained to feel. Feeling different though wasn't a privileged feeling. I felt oddly different. The children never made fun of me though - It was quite the contrary. They invited me to play at their homes and to share the treats there. Those innocent kids didn't know that I was being taught that anyone who was not walking with Jehovah was walking with Satan. Because their parents were not Witnesses they were automatically wicked.

It was completely forbidden to participate in any extracurricular activities because we were not allowed to socialize with non-Witness children after school. So I always made up excuses as to why I couldn't come over to play. That was a lonely feeling because my sisters and I were also outcasts at the Kingdom Hall. I will explain this experience shortly.

The worst part of this time of the year was how we were schooled to "take our stand" and push our religious agenda onto the teachers and the classmates. The **School Brochure** magazine was what we placed to explain the holiday origins and why we didn't celebrate them and why they shouldn't celebrate them either. I think all Witness children would have had an awesome career in public speaking and being sales people because we were trained unbelievably well.

It embarrassed me that it wasn't enough to simply leave the class room during the holidays. No, we had to preach. We had to witness. We had to separate the sheep from the goat. We were also required to write down each hour that we spent preaching and each piece of literature that we placed.

I remember that, in those days, we charged fifty cent to one dollar for the literature depending on what was placed. Let me repeat this: "We" charged "You" for the literature that "We" brought to "Your" door and this literature was supposed to be given to you by an organization who was directly guided by god. I'll leave that where it is and allow that to sink in for a moment.

Taking your stand meant that you had to completely separate yourself from anything or anyone who did not share your faith. It also meant that you had to give your life to the Watchtower organization which was emphasized in part of the last baptismal question for those becoming baptized Jehovah's Witnesses. Anything you did must be approved by them. The movies you went to see, the music you listened to, all the way to the entertainment you chose - all had to be Watchtower approved. Association with non-Witnesses could actually get you disfellowshipped if you continued to do so. They truly had control over each member of its congregations using their greatest weapons: fear and mind control.

Chapter 3

Separated by Economic Status

Not being able to associate with non-Witnesses was more than enough torture because conveying hatred toward the only people that showed any real concern or friendship, just because they were not of my faith, was pretty doggone coldhearted. So now school became a playground for guilt, yet after turning down play dates, time and again, these kids never showed any hatred. They were confused and at times they seemed downright hurt. I knew, deep in my heart, that this was cruel but by then the brainwashing began to set in so I figured that this was a necessary evil in order to please Jehovah and live forever.

However the real torture came from the kids at the Kingdom Hall which is the place of worship for the Jehovah's Witnesses. Everyone pretty much belonged to different cliques. Most of the cliques were formed according to what appeared to be the financial status of each kid based on what they wore to the hall and to school.

My family lived in a pretty big house in the suburbs. Our neighbors were of many different ethnicities and shades and religious beliefs. Though we all boasted a familiar economic background based upon where we lived, I would later find out that, many of us were struggling beyond belief. In fact my siblings and I wore mostly hand-me-downs. The bad part was that they were given to us from other kids at the hall. How humiliating!

My father made good money, at least good enough to keep us living in a middle class suburb, so why we went without so much was a mystery that fortunately I don't care to solve anymore. The scars, however, of never being invited to parties by anyone always left a mark on me.

Picture this: My mother decided that we should have a party of our own and invite the kids from the congregation because she thought that we should widen our association within the congregation. So we did just that. A few adults came to assists with the food preparations. One hour later no one showed. Two hours later no one showed. Three hours later no one showed. We gave up because four hours later still no one showed. I saw the utter disappointment and sadness in my eldest sister's face. I wanted to cry for her. Is there any wonder why we were so reserved?

This type of treatment instilled low self-esteem in me, among other things. This treatment coupled with the daily reminders that our everlasting life or death depended upon our every thought and action, set me up at a young age to start having anxiety and panic disorders. So now I became very afraid, almost to an obsession, about any thought that I had that wasn't in sync with the Watchtower organization would cause me to die.

For this reason, every Christmas song I sang in silence made me reek with fear. Every Halloween candy I accepted and ate sure enough would get me killed. At times though I think I would have accepted the consequences just to get a feel of the fun that the other kids were having.

My Book of Bible Stories did not help. Seeing pictures of babies being destroyed by natural forces caused me to have an intense fear of thunder and lightning. I'd joke around sometimes about how the lightning wouldn't kill us and laugh. That gave me a very short moment of strength until the next crashing sound of thunder and the room illuminating lightening would come upon us. My first thought was that I just caused Armageddon to come and everyone who laughed and joked about the lightning would be killed. This was a sincere fear. What I failed to realize was that the thunder was just as loud and earth shattering before I made my joke, so I wasn't being punished. I didn't know any better.

I think if I brought this up to my sisters now we would all have a pretty good laugh. I know they remember how I'd shake like a fall leaf and hide under my mother's arms or under her blanket. As a matter of fact as soon as the weather man gave a thunderstorm warning I would began to shake and watch for any sign of lightning. My sincere fear was not of the storm itself, but of Armageddon.

I only started to deal with my panic attacks and anxiety without medication about two years ago. As of this writing I have come a very long way. I still suffer to a big degree but it's nowhere near as crippling as it used to be. Thankfully, I no longer have the same fears and issues that I had in the past.

Unfortunately, having a disfellowshipped father only added fuel to the mental torture. What was designed to keep our family clean and in good standing with God would only prove to assassinate our family ties. To this day I am still trying to "fully" resuscitate my strained relationship with my father.

Chapter 4

The Effects of Having a Disfellowshipped Parent

I have no recollection of my father's name being called off at the hall as being disfellowshipped but I do remember my mother telling my siblings and me that this would happen. Even though I had no idea why, as I was only about eight years old when I was told. I still remember feeling like my father would be taken away from me. The irony of it is that my father never seemed to be home to begin with.

As time went on resentment for my father grew greater and greater as I became more aware of his absence. In fact he seemed happier living away from home. I remember one day my sister took out a box full of photos that my mother kept and we both began to look through the photos to find recent pictures of our father to remember what he looked like. I will never forget that moment.

As my resentment grew so did the ever annoying conversations about my father being bad association and how we were to limit our contact with him to business matters only. Since at times seemed oblivious to us I began to believe that perhaps he was bad association. I also began to believe that he didn't love us enough. This made me cling to my mother with all of my might.

During these early years after his disfellowshipping I remember feeling like we were inherently defective children. People made it perfectly clear that because we were now officially part of a broken home, somehow we are flawed. No one knew how lonely I was at this tender age and how badly their words hurt me but I internalized every pitiful stare given to us and every pitiful word said about us.

My mother spoiled me like no one else could. She made me feel beautiful and worthy although it wasn't a replacement for my father but for a while it came close. I felt beautiful and worthy because she always told me how beautiful and smart I was. I felt an unwavering sense of security around my mother.

I started getting used to having only one parent around. In fact, for a little while, it actually felt weird though still refreshing when we did visit my father and when he did take us to annual events. My favorite time with my father was going to the city's annual River Fest. This would also be one of the only memories aside from a few others, that I remember spending quality time with him.

It is my present belief that had my father never became a Jehovah's Witness, I would have had a more attentive and affectionate father growing up. I think he would have recognized my teenage rebellious appearances as a sign of something bigger instead of making fun of me both publicly and privately. I don't think he would have been so critical. I don't think I would have felt the need to figuratively jump in front of a train to gain his approval and love. Perhaps none of these things would have been an issue.

As a teenager I used to wonder why he didn't seem to have any authority over anything that happened to us as far as decision making. I do remember being very upset that we could not at least attend school in his suburban neighborhood but instead we had to attend one of the worst schools in the inner city that my mother had to move us to. I would be an adult when I would finally understand that the non-custodial parent wasn't allowed as much freedom to make final decisions, especially against the will of the custodial parent.

The price paid for my father being disfellowshipped was pathetic. My siblings and I were now considered bad association. I've heard this about us throughout the years. As time progressed me and one of my sisters were constantly accused of thinking we were too cute and that we thought too much of ourselves. My mother would actually suffer the same trash talk about her because she really was beautiful. She was beautiful in a "drop dead gorgeous" kind of way. She was counseled about her lack of parenting skills because my sister and I began to very quietly date non-Witness boys. It's funny though because all of the kids who had fathers, especially the fathers who were elders, were worse than the "worldly" kids.

They had the Sodom and Gomorrah lifestyle down to a science.

I was never envious or ashamed not to have my father present because we lived this way for so long that it became normal. I wouldn't realize until much later that my father was all I wanted and I suffered something awful without him. We all did. We just expressed it in different ways. Without even realizing it until later, I used "the truth" against him to soothe my hurt for feeling unloved by him. The "truth" was my figurative alcohol to medicate my hurt.

I now know that my father loved us unconditionally but it was difficult to see it then because he was so stern and often times very belittling and that's exactly how I received it. What he saw as a father's way of showing love was counterproductive because, coupled with his constant absence, it made him look mean and ashamed to me. Deep down though I knew we had done nothing too shameful or wrong. Eventually however, I began to feel that he only felt ashamed of me. I was constantly told that his absence was because he didn't love Jehovah. I was constantly told that when he was walking with Jehovah he was the best father a kid could have. I was constantly told that he wouldn't feel comfortable around me because I am a faithful servant of Jehovah and we have nothing in common. I was told a lot but no one ever told me how this may have affected him, as well.

I never realized nor did I care at the time that this man very well could have been in pain. When I did find out why he was disfellowshipped I cared very much that his actions broke a lot of hearts and a beautiful home. I was mad because being selfish took him away from us and being disfellowshipped kept him away. In other words he seemed to be less and less invested in us.

Only after leaving the organization would I begin to not only forgive my father but also gain insight about what struggles he may have endured as a result of realizing that this was not the truth, having a wife who was a devout member of the organization, choosing between leaving my mother to escape a lie, or staying with the lie to stay with my mother, and being shunned by so-called friends and family. Absolutely nothing can excuse being selfish because of some inner or outward conflict, but I do understand how even a good person can make a horrible, and for some an irreversible, mistake when their back was against the wall.

For the time being, I turned to the elders especially for that fatherly attention. They always told me how proud I made Jehovah by shunning my father. They made me feel validated for all the wrong reasons but as sure as this organization had molded me into the robotic follower I was trained to be from infancy, was as sure as these same men would cause me to, initially, second guess this religion.

Chapter 5

Emotional Rape by the Elders

By now I was about 19 years old. I was pregnant with my first child out of wedlock, though I would soon marry the father. I felt so unclean and so ashamed. Nevertheless my mother was once again my greatest support system. She was looking forward to having what would be her second grandchild.

After hearing my father tell me that I would never amount to anything while we sat in his car at the park, to having my soon to be husband cheat on me like it was nothing, I began to seek out confirmation from wherever I could get it. The same source that I began to look to for approval would become the same source that would humiliate me in a way that no person should be humiliated for confessing a sin.

There were three elders alone with me. We were in a small room where all private committee meetings are held. As I observed how they wrote down what appeared to be everything I said, I confessed in detail my sin of fornication. It began when one elder asked me who initiated the act. I paused out of shock. They then directed me to a scripture about keeping the organization clean. They then reminded me that I would bring reproach on Jehovah and his organization if I didn't answer all of their questions truthfully. So I very reluctantly told them that my boyfriend initiated the act. Another elder asked me if we had oral sex. Yet another elder asked me what positions we were in and who took off the clothing. The last perverse question was if I enjoyed it. I'm having a hard time even writing this now.

Needless to say I answered all of these questions because my young mind was afraid and didn't know any better. I only knew that I'd probably die from fornicating but if I wanted a chance to redeem myself I needed to spill the beans in full and get my act together. They decided to publicly reprove me which is a mild equivalent to being disfellowshipped. People could still talk to me but I couldn't participate in any parts of the meeting or go from door to door. Looking back, I should have been happy but I couldn't be after feeling like I was verbally raped by those elders.

From that moment on I never felt comfortable going to the hall. Not that particular congregation and not for a long time coming. These elders had all of the verbal ammunition to enjoy that meeting shy of having an actual video of the situation. I will never forgive them for that. Never!

When I finally left the organization I wrote a letter to those elders telling them how badly they had messed my head up but that I had the power to overcome it and heal from it. I wish that kind of humiliation on no one, unfortunately mind control took control of me.

Chapter 6

In the Name of the Father

(Fear was instilled)

Jehovah God created the heavens and the earth. Everything he made was perfect. He had perfect angels that he created to reside in heaven with him. He then created a perfect man and called him Adam. Adam was to help cultivate the ground and name the animals. Jehovah, however, saw that Adam was lonely so he created a companion for him. From the rib of Adam he created a woman whom he named Eve.

God gave them the entire Garden of Eden to enjoy with the exception of one tree, the tree of the knowledge of good and bad. He commanded them not to touch that tree for in the day they would eat from it they would positively die. Then comes along a talking snake who temps Eve and, in turn, Eve temps Adam and they eat.

Assuming that most people are familiar with what that story says are consequences suffered as a result of Adam and Eve's disobedience, I would like to share how Fear of Jehovah was instilled in me from infancy.

Jehovah used the flood to wash away all disobedient mankind. In a graphic description of this event, the *My Book of Bible Stories* illustrates how tiny babies, as well as children, were being swallowed up in the flood waters. They were dying because of the actions of their parents. That served later on as an extra strike against my disfellowshipped father. It was also told to me that if your parents didn't have the correct heart condition it would be apparent by their lack of activity at the Kingdom Hall. Because of this their children would inherit the same heart condition and would lose their lives with their parents in Armageddon. These images gave me a morbid fear of Jehovah.

We learned that Jehovah had promised not to flood the earth again and the rainbow serves as a reminder of his promise. Instead he would use all other natural forces such as fire, hail, lightning, etc., to destroy the wicked, which would include those mentioned above. So every bad occurrence in the news that happens to a "worldly" person was a result of not serving Jehovah. Every war, every gruesome murder, every report of famine, or disease was a sign that Armageddon was around the corner. By the way, it has been around the corner since 1914. That's just food for thought that I myself only began to chew on after my exit.

Now picture being told and being shown these things for as long as you can remember. Other children your age are reading *Green Eggs and Ham* while you're reading all of the horrible things a kid your age could die for. Other kids have illustrations of Mickey and Minnie or some other happy cartoon characters dancing around while you have illustrations of kids and babies hanging on to a big rock with their mommies waiting for the waters and lightning to come and kill them. As a kid you were forbidden to watch the Smurfs but we were allowed to read the bible story book about God killing children. Let that sink in for a moment.

The fear tactics worked though. I became afraid of my thoughts, my actions, and pretty much anything that didn't come from the Watchtower Society as they often called it. Since Jehovah was aware of my thoughts, as well, I knew that even a thought about why God seemed so mean, might and probably, would get me killed. I still wondered periodically. What an exhausting childhood! What a confusing and anxious childhood!

Soon panic attacks and anxiety would rule my life though at the time, of course, I wasn't aware of what exactly was happening to me. I would sweat and my heart would beat through my shirt whenever I walked passed people. I thought that people were laughing at me or judging me for no apparent reason. I wanted to hide under a rock forever when I came to the door of a classmate in the ministry because I'd be afraid that they would make fun of me. If I dared harbor any thoughts of shame I would change them to the best of my ability so I wouldn't make Jehovah angry. I existed in the name of the Father out of pure fear. Again, what an exhausting childhood!

Chapter 7

In the Name of the Son

(Nothing was Instilled)

Interestingly enough Jehovah's Witnesses just began to put any real emphasis on Jesus in recent years. Jesus was always passively mentioned. In fact, the Watchtower organization received more attention than Jesus did. The focus was always on Jehovah's name and the fact that the religion used Jehovah's name in their title. So the majority of the focus was on being sure that we did nothing to bring reproach on Jehovah's organization. Of course that would be the Watchtower, as well.

At the Kingdom Hall the elders tell the audience what scriptures to turn to. They would then read only the verse(s) or phrase(s) within a verse that they wanted you to see. Then they would explain "their" interpretation of the scriptures, usually starting with: "So, you see brothers and sisters, this is plainly telling us"..., or something to that affect. Of course their interpretation was the only correct interpretation according to them because they were directly guided by Jehovah's Holy Spirit.

That said, I never actually knew that Jesus had anything to do directly with the earth's creation. I definitely didn't know that he was also the Alpha and Omega, the first and the last. This is the case at least in Revelation 22:13 where Jesus is plainly speaking of himself. It's also 21:6. Ironically in Revelation 1:8 Jehovah god says the same thing about himself. In case anyone is wondering these scriptures are found in the New World Translation used only by Jehovah's Witnesses.

I could have sworn that Jehovah never gave his authority to anyone else as Jesus says that "he" is the one coming and the reward is with "him" in Revelation 22:12. Please forgive my lack of capitalization for the word god and him, as I am currently speaking in a baffled state of mind.

The Jehovah's Witnesses describe the Trinity as a belief in some three headed god. I however, take issue with the fact that I am seeing Jesus being described as obviously the same deity as god. I don't care what scriptures show him speaking to god and praying to god, there are still many more scriptures that outright convey that he is indeed god. I personally do not care if they are the same or not because that won't guarantee my eternal life and I will not gain extra points towards living forever regardless. I do say that if they are the same it does not mean that god has three heads. It makes more sense that he would be one god with three distinct roles.

The example that comes to my mind is the thought of a male child being born. This child automatically becomes the son of someone. Let's call him John Doe. John Doe grows up and decides he wants to get married. John Doe is still the same person and he is still a son of someone. Now however he is also a husband. He now has two distinct titles but he is the same person. Now John Doe becomes a father. John is the same exact person with three distinct titles and functions or roles. John Doe is a father, son and husband. The same would apply to the Trinity if it were real.

As a Jehovah's Witness I had no real appreciation for Jesus. He seemed like a side kick for God. To speak on the importance of Jesus would take away from the importance of the name "Jehovah." This is the religion's identifying mark.

I absolutely learned nothing of Jesus' importance (unless it was the annual memorial celebration of the death of Jesus) until I began to read the bible independent of the religion. This "independent thinking" has always been and continues to be frowned upon. By the time they began to speak of Jesus regularly I had already formed enough questions and doubts so that in a meeting I was listening for contradictions and not the truth anymore. Even if Jesus had been mentioned daily it seems odd that they do some cold hearted stuff such as shunning, that Jesus would never do. So unfortunately Jesus made no real impact on me or at least not until my exit.

Chapter 8

In the Name of the Watchtower

(Hatred and Intolerance Instilled)

This is the part of my life that was the game changer. Love for the Watchtower taught me a lot about differences. It made it absolutely clear that being different was the identifying mark of a godly person.

Now let me clarify something. I'm not speaking of the sort of different that makes us individuals. I'm not speaking of the sort of different that we teach our children to be because we want them to be strong enough to avoid peer pressure and we want them to be leaders and not followers and to think for themselves. The different that the Watchtower speaks of and essentially trains its members to be is "completely separated" from the rest of the world. I mean that very literally.

Being completely separated means that as a Jehovah's Witness you may not associate with non-Witnesses outside of work or school hours for any sort of recreational activities.

You may not join in discussions at any time with non-Witnesses unless it involved preaching to them about Jehovah. Your children may not be involved in extracurricular activities after school. You could not celebrate holidays and if someone extended a gift to you, it could only be accepted before or after the said holiday. You could not attend concerts. You could not eat with non-Witnesses out of pure friendship unless the gathering involved preaching to them about Jehovah. You could not have casual friendships, especially close friendships, with non-Witnesses. Television programs, movies, music and even cartoons had to fall under the guidelines of what was appropriate for witnesses.

Any form of entertainment had fall under the guideline of what was appropriate for Witnesses. You better not ever accept and read any other religious material. You absolutely better run from a book like this one here. If you even vaguely entertained a book like this one you might as well prepare to be shunned or wish that you were shunned by the time everyone gets through with you.

Now one might wonder how tabs are kept on all of the members of each congregation. It is quite simple actually. By a certain point every congregation has its fair share of brainwashed followers. These followers have a lot to do with information being reported back to the congregation elders. For example, if you are a young adult and one of your parents has become a devout member of the organization and they learned that you have attended a concert of some sort. Not only would they reprimand you themselves, they would call elders over to have a meeting with you. This is because they feel that it is their duty to Jehovah to keep his organization clean.

This means that for the love of the Watchtower organization and not necessarily for God, yes, your very own family members would turn you in and, if advised by the elders, they would turn against you if you appeared unrepentant for your actions. Simply associating with non-Witnesses can get you disfellowshipped or publicly reproved or punished publicly.

An offense that was worse than any of the above mentioned offenses was speaking to someone who was disfellowshipped. These individuals may or may not have voluntarily left the organization but nonetheless they were read off in front of the congregation as being disfellowshipped. This means that at no time is any witness ever allowed to speak with this person even if it's your own child unless it involves business matters or if there is a life and death matter. Ironically, relating to disfellowshipped individuals, you are not allowed to speak to them about Jehovah.

To this very day I do not understand for the life of me why a person who is disfellowshipped would be exempt from bible discussions. If anything, it seems that the person would benefit from bible discussions - if they actually did something wrong. If a witness is caught speaking to a disfellowshipped person on a continued basis they will be disfellowshipped and shunned worse than the person they were associating with.

All of these rules of complete separation reminds me of the civil rights era when blacks and whites were separated because of the belief that colored people were somehow inferior. That's the exact mentality of this so-called "spiritual" separation. This mentality is ingrained in the minds of infants and young vulnerable children. It is, also, very easy to mislead vulnerable individuals, such as single mothers or people having hardships, into believing everything about this organization. This is the audience that is preyed upon most easily.

The Jehovah's Witnesses come to a person's door to offer all sorts of hope to people who are feeling very hopeless. They make you feel so welcome and so loved just long enough to get you into a good bible study routine. Once the person has begun studying for at least four to six months, then the pressure begins to set in.

By now this person has already been taught that they were living in total sin their entire lives. The pressure to prove that one is serious about changing their life around to worship god correctly must now take place in the form of regular meeting attendance and studying for the five weekly congregation meetings. At this point the pressure is felt. This is the point when people give in and the brainwashing is evident.

Suddenly everyone around you that you previously viewed as just another human being becomes "worldly." They can no longer serve any further purpose in your life because they are of Satan's world. In fact they are dangerous to your spiritual health. They are bad association because they are not "like minded." If they had a receptive heart then they would recognize immediately that the only true organization is the Watchtower organization. They would receive your message, believe your message, and act upon your message if their heart condition was right. All of this separation teaches the brainwashed member to show hate to anyone who is not a Jehovah's Witness.

I became one of those brainwashed people at the time in my life when I was looking for acceptance and when it seemed that my life had hit rock bottom. I stopped speaking to the very people who had never judged me but in fact encouraged me the most, just because they were not Witnesses. I knew, deep down, I felt like I had committed the worst betrayal but I learned to quickly blow that feeling off and chalked it up as another one of Satan's tactics to try to discourage me. Pretty soon it became second nature for me to judge people all around me. Even though I was sinning for judging others I couldn't tell. I was an effectively trained member of the rank and file at the kingdom hall of Jehovah's Witnesses directed by God through the Watchtower organization.

Chapter 9

Double Standards Instilled - but Not for Long

As I began to increase my participation in the door to door ministry I also began increasing my thirst for the gossip that the pioneer sisters would bring into the car ride each day. This was great entertainment. I had a full view of the supposed lives of many members of the congregation. This just added fuel to give me more of a reason to judge people. It put me on some sort of power trip. It was like having free unlimited tickets to the Wendy Williams show.

Being trained by the Watchtower also taught me double standards. I learned the art of double standard thinking down to a science. I could clearly see that a lot of people in the local congregations were actually doing worse things than non-Witnesses. However carrying the name Jehovah's Witness seemed to give some the idea that they were automatically extended a free pass to sin willfully.

I would learn in my late teens and early twenties that two of the elders who were responsible for having my father disfellowshipped were themselves committing adultery against their own wives. One of the elders committed adultery with an active pioneer sister. The brothers, in general, had sticky eyes, if you will. They had their eyes stuck on a lot of the sisters in the hall, married or not. Of course the temptation was in plain view because the sisters were notorious for wearing skirts above the knees with six inch stilettos - especially during the annual district and circuit conventions.

These conventions that gathered Witnesses from around the country and often times from around the world were supposed to give everyone a grand spiritual awakening or refreshment. Instead these conventions put a huge stress on poor people who could not compete in what appeared to be a mandatory fashion show. Of course this particular behavior was not Watchtower induced or indorsed, but the Witnesses seemed to make up this particular activity along the way so everyone who was able seemed to participate, willingly or reluctantly.

Anywhere that there is an entrance or exit there will be contribution boxes. Thousands upon thousands of people donate money for the so-called printing costs of the materials that they gave to the members for personal studies and to place with people in the door to door preaching work. The *Watchtower* and *Awake* magazines continued to be the most popular but nowhere near the only literature used or placed by a long shot. I will speak a lot more about this particular subject of contributions when I talk about my exit from the religion.

During my teenage years I witnessed some of the worst kinds of behaviors among the Witness youths. These were the only kids I was allowed to play with yet I witnessed verbal battery, physical fights, the foulest of foul language, drug dealing, alcoholism at its worst, fornication, drug use, provocative attire and mannerisms, and degrading and violent music choices just to name the majority though not all of what I witnessed. It got so bad at the congregations that were in the same area as mine - I honestly thought the doors would be chained up some day.

The youths seemed to enjoy this lifestyle. I judged them so harshly but looking back on it now I realize that we were all caged animals. Try releasing a lion from a cage that he has been confined to forever and see how it behaves. Hence the reckless behaviors of the Witness youths in very large portions, so large in fact that I have to be very careful not to generalize. Please understand that I do not condone these behaviors but I do understand it now. I can honestly say that I get it.

I began to view the world and everyone in it with a fine toothed comb. I had noticed that the more I showed intolerance and the more I judged people the more the older members of the congregation began to make me feel important. I actually had a huge sense of belonging and that was super powerful. I belonged inside of these four walls that were prearranged just for me. These four walls gave me open access to what was available within only these four walls.

As I grew older however, this sense of security, of belonging and of power began to fade consistently. I also grew increasingly uncomfortable with the idea of congregational status giving some people a free pass to sin incessantly and to be able to do the same things that others would get disfellowshipped for without a second thought. I really began to realize just how unhappy I was all along.

Chapter 10

Mental Withdrawal Out of the Watchtower and Into the Real World

Real world issues became a part of my life. I realized that I now had to interact with the world. These four walls don't help to pay rent or put food on the table. These four walls won't take my child to the ER when she starts having severe asthma attacks. These four walls encourage me not to pursue higher education to pay my bills more easily.

It was because of this realization that a series of severe panic attacks that would last indefinitely became a part of my daily life. Because I had separated myself in such an extreme way, I feared being around that which was very uncomfortable, normal people. Notice I didn't say "people" I said "normal people".

I thought that everyone was laughing at me or staring at me. I thought people wanted to hurt me. For some reason it also seemed like the entire world knew that I was a Witness so they were laughing at me. I had great difficulty interacting with normal beings. I may or may not have hidden it well but it was one of my greatest struggles to date. The more fear that I felt the more evil I felt these people were. At times I would avoid dealing with people altogether.

I began to pray to Jehovah for strength and guidance to help me to cope with this very uncomfortable state of being. It did relieve some stress for a moment - but not nearly enough to alleviate the situation or to stop my panic attacks from occurring so frequently. I began to read the bible more and more just to gain some strength from it but I "hated" that book. It was boring. It was unappealing. It made very little sense even though I had accepted it as fact all of these years. I had accepted that logic is not a trait of God. He was too perfect to be a logical being. The bible actually induced my anxiety especially the book of Revelation. It brought not an ounce of comfort to me regardless of the great façade that I put on.

I knew nothing else though. I only knew what I was taught and what I was allowed to be exposed to. I couldn't just stop believing because that would essentially take away any purpose or meaning of my life. I decided at this point, with caution, to continue to put my trust in Jehovah by following his spirit anointed organization. Now, if the last sentence that I just wrote could be heard, you would have heard my voice drag alone in a low depressing monotone because that's exactly how I felt about it at this point.

All of these years of hatred and intolerance would come back onto me with a vengeance. It would overtake my mental health so much that eventually I had to seek professional help and from there I was clinically diagnosed with depression, panic disorder, and generalized anxiety with an emphasis on social anxiety. I was in my early to mid-twenties at this point. I never achieved the level of success that I should have been capable of, not only because it was discouraged but also because I was afraid. I don't mean a normal fear. I mean a very abnormal fear that causes a room to spin, dizzy spells, anything that was not normal.

I do realize that mental illness is largely hereditary so being in this restrictive and fear induced environment was a disastrous recipe for a problem that probably already existed but that spiraled out of control from living in fear of the wrath of god and the constant fear of dying from all of his natural forces over even something as petty as a thought. To realize that the love from the members of the congregation was conditional and only extended to those who worshipped the Watchtower, and only for as long as they worshipped it, definitely made matters worse.

The minute real life happened and inactivity from the meetings and the door to door preaching became evident, the love stops. Suddenly a harsh reminder of how it feels to be judged slaps you dead in your face. The love stops. You are no longer exempt from judgment and as readily as your free pass was given - it was readily taken.

It was at this point in my life that my face said that I was happy but my heart and my mind were at war. My mind kept telling me that Satan is getting the best of me. I need to change my association immediately although I was only in association with Witnesses, at least, for the most part. I must be doing something wrong. I was a servant of the only true God. I would know to lean on Jehovah no matter how bad it gets and lean on the brothers and sisters for guidance. Continue to meditate on the endless droves of magazines, books, audios and videos for strength and encouragement. My heart was telling me that I was not in a comfortable place. It was telling me to ask questions later but to "Get Out Now!" I hung on to my brainwashed mind in complete misery.

At this point the only thing that kept me from leaving and continuing to make excuses against myself as to why I'm suddenly feeling so rotten, is the fear of losing all of my loved ones in the religion, fear of a brutal and unforgiving death in the form of unadulterated torture IF I am wrong about leaving, and last, but actually primarily, the fear of displeasing my mother.

Chapter 11

Choosing Torture Out of Fear

This has got to be what proved to be my greatest downfall in life. There was no way that I could disappoint my mother. She was my number one and probably my only ally during my worst times. She was essentially my mother and my father. To betray her by even entertaining the thought of leaving the organization would be hateful on my part. I owed her at least that much.

To this minute my mother is one of the most extreme Jehovah's Witnesses. In her mind, to question the religion would be complete betrayal. My happiness didn't exist. I never even really knew what made me happy or what I wanted in life. All I knew was making my mother happy and what she wanted for me and from me out of life. I was the youngest child and therefore the closest to my mother so when my siblings broke away it was hard for my mother but not for them. They seemed more disappointed in upsetting our father. Maybe this was a way of gaining and holding on to any level of approval from someone who could be so critical. They have memories that I do not. They remember when my father was home daily. They remember when my father seemed happy and whole. I have no recollection of that part of life hence my fear of disappointing my mother only.

So with this I continued to attend meetings but consistently becoming less and less active. I'd sit at the hall wondering why others seemed to be blessed but I was not. I also noticed that the elders who spoke against materialism had the latest and greatest suits and cars and homes and businesses. Their wives wore flashy attire. They usual drove in separate expensive cars. These were the ones who appeared so happy. But I noticed that there were those like me who were just barely smiling on the outside but crumbling on the inside. These were the single moms like me who were either deserted by their husbands, like I was, or who never married. These were the ones who had to swallow their pride week after week and ask for a ride for them and all of their young kids. When they became a burden on the current driver, the responsibility was passed on to someone else and so on.

I began to sit at the hall not to learn because nothing I've heard thus far was helping to resolve this wicked mental illness hiding inside of my head but instead I began to keep track of anything debatable, anything contradicting. That wasn't a hard task because more often than not the organization would change their previous views on things. It was much easier to say that god gave them "new light" instead of just saying that they were wrong.

Week after week, month after month, year after year I sat quietly at the hall whenever excuses not to attend just didn't cut it. If I missed two or more meetings in a row the people from the hall would come over unannounced and see what was keeping me away from the hall. At the end of every visit the reminder that my life was on the line, backed by scripture after scripture was thrown in my face. I preferred to just sit quietly at the back of the hall so that at least my home could be free. I also tortured myself just to avoid disappointing my mother. It's shameful that a person or an entity could have so much power over a person but it happens and quite often.

Chapter 12

Prepare to Leave Now; Count the Costs (if any) Later

When I am told that going to the Salvation Army for food is a bad thing because it is a religious organization, but I can't get help to pay my rent or electric bill or put food upon my table except by a few dedicated and good natured individuals when they were able to at their discretion, yet when I do finally visit the Salvation Army these people give me a month's worth of food, help to keep my utilities on, pay my rent, give the children gifts at any time just because and do this on a monthly basis all without speaking to me about their obvious religion affiliation - something needs to be pondered seriously.

I'm supposed to hate the hands that feed me and love the hands that don't? I'm supposed to reject the people who feed me without conditions and love the people who won't feed me but will be cool with me under certain conditions? This is what the bible says? Ok, just a minute here something is missing right?

Fear of a tortured death and fear of losing my mother kept me unhappily attending the meetings, even instilling into my children that this was the truth. I had to be sure to cover them just in case I was wrong because I didn't want them to die because of my thoughts. But I also began to dip my toes into the waters of ex-Jehovah's Witnesses and their stories over the internet. If I didn't know any better I'd swear I wrote everyone's story across the globe. How can all of our situations, questions, concerns, fears and pains be almost and in some cases completely identical? That is NOT coincidental. There was something to this.

But again fear kept stalling me from the inevitable. It worked until my mother's very own words was the straw the broke the camel's back. She has no idea that it was her unloving words towards another ex-Witness human being that was practically blood that saved my life very literally. It forced me not to care too much anymore and to research this organization that took over my life so badly that at certain points I could actually fathom suicide. I never would have thought I could fathom suicide but I came to that point. My mother's lack of love put the key in my hand to release me from incarceration.

Chapter 13

My Search for the Real Truth

I moved my mother in with me for a year or so. During that time, in my very own home, I began sneaking around and started independently researching not only the Jehovah's Witness religion but all religions. I wanted to see just how different Jehovah's Witnesses were or were not from the other religions. What I found actually allowed me to stop taking Prozac for depression because I would learn very quickly just how false and even dangerous this religion was and is and has proven to be. So I felt pretty certain that my death was not so imminent anymore.

Still with a touch of uncertainty I decided that if it was appropriate for disciples in the bible to pray to God almost in a demanding tone then certainly with a humble heart I could approach God in prayer and tell him what he should already know that I'm feeling. So this is what I did. I told God that I "hate" going to the kingdom hall and that the bible teaches me to fear Him instead of to trust Him and to love Him. I told Him that all I desired was the truth no matter how brutal and that I'd rather die being wrong but sincere in truly searching for Him than to stay with an organization with an angry heart just to die anyway. I kid you not that immediately after I said "Amen" my fear was erased for the first time in my life ever.

I opened up the bible - the book that I could never enjoy because I could never really grasp it - and suddenly it appeared interesting. I started form Genesis and I saw the bible in a way that didn't seem possible. I actually started to feel closer to a spirit. The bible was next to me in the morning and next to me at bedtime. The things to be revealed about this religion would prove to be a life changing experience of overwhelming proportions. I felt resentment because of all of the pseudo hope that was extended to me in the name of this religion but I felt relief. The relief was overwhelming - it was all happening so fast.

Life was set and ready to begin. Now with total freedom from fear of death and without fear of disappointing my mother, I present to you the information that finally led me to my freedom from the Watchtower organization in August of 2010.

Chapter 14

What the Watchtower Doesn't Want You to Know

Ever wonder why Jesus directed his disciples to call upon God in prayer as Father and not Jehovah? (Matthew 6: 5-13) Has it even occurred to you that Jesus himself never called God by the name Jehovah anywhere in the bible? Were you aware that the Witnesses who were formerly known as Bible Students, celebrated Christmas until the late 1920's or to be exact, December 12, 1928? Birthday celebrations continued until 1951.

The bible students who would later be called Jehovah's Witnesses were founded by Charles Taze Russell. He began going to Adventists meetings but when disagreement arose concerning dates of when the world was going to end, Russell showed interest in keeping the newly founded Seventh Day Adventist organization alive because so many became discouraged over failed prophecies. So the origin of this religion began with a religion that they will tell you is false.

Other things to take note of is that for over 40 years the Watchtower used the cross, taught that Jesus died on a cross and used the cross on the cover of the Watch Tower magazines until the 1930's when J. F. Rutherford took over the Watchtower society following Russell's death. The exact removal date was October 15, 1931. Rutherford began to promote the views of several Protestant preachers. According to them the cross was introduced by Constantine in an effort to make Christianity more appealing to the Pagans who were already using the cross as a symbol. In their book called **The Harp of God** on page 141, Rutherford stated that "The cross of Christ is the greatest pivotal truth of divine arrangement, from which radiate the hopes of men."

How ironic it is that the Watchtower changed their view of the cross completely! In the May 1, 1989 Watchtower on page 23, the Watchtower warns that "There are also inanimate objects that if venerated (worshipped) may lead to breaking God's commandments. Among the most prominent is the cross. For centuries it has been used by people in Christendom as part of their worship. Soon God will execute his judgments against all false religions. Those who cling to them will suffer their fate." This is the current belief of the Watchtower regarding the cross.

These are just a few of the doctrine that have changed over time because according to the Watchtower Jehovah shed new light on the way they should worship him. The reason why I present to you even a fraction of the origin of this religion is to show that their argument about avoiding holiday's and other pagan practices based on the previous or current origin or reason of practice, would prove that they fit into the category in which they condemn to judgment and God's wrath.

If any part of the origin of this religion was founded upon any other religious beliefs or practices then the origin of this religion is pagan. The Watchtower began in 1879 and the official use of the name Jehovah's Witnesses began in 1931. Why would God wait so long to suddenly have his chosen people to start using his name? Why would his chosen people still operate under the direction of a pagan entity, The Watchtower? Surely God's chosen people would have known that these holiday's and other practices were pagan because he is supposed to "directly" guide his organization.

Concerning child molestation, the Witnesses require two or more witnesses before taking private action against the accused. This would mean that two or more victims would have to come forward OR the accused would have to confess. That in itself is problematic. If even one person comes to any entity with accusations of being molested this should always be investigated.

The worst however is that Jehovah's Witnesses do not favor going to law enforcement at all because they are trying to protect the reputation of the organization. Public knowledge of any gross sin would be bringing reproach upon the organization. There are people that I know personally who have been silenced after being molested and in most cases repeatedly. This is an organization who is supposed to follow the laws of the land so long as they do not conflict with God's laws. The law says that crimes are supposed to be reported to the proper authorities. I wonder what makes them claim an exemption status!

I had a thought one evening and I suddenly realized that the entire time that I attended the meetings, whenever there was a change in something or whenever a letter that was deemed important enough to share was read before the congregation, we were always told that the information comes straight from the Society. That word "society" is used today more than even when I was a child. For some reason the words Secret Society came to mind. It felt eerie to even think about. What was more interesting however was that even upon my exit from the organization, society or whatever one may choose to call it, I found myself defending the organization from those claiming it to be a cult. So at this time even as a new ex-Witness I would become livid for someone calling the religion a cult.

Chapter 15

If It Walks Like a Cult, Talks Like a Cult, Feels Like a Cult…

Until one day I found myself in a debate with someone on this subject. I decided to Google the definition and signs of a cult just to prove this person wrong. This would prove to be the awakening that I needed that in fact proved me wrong. While reading the signs of a religious cult it described Jehovah's Witnesses down to the letter. For anyone even slightly familiar with the religion, these signs will ring a bell. For anyone in the process of becoming a witness or who is already an active witness this information I'm about to address should alarm you unless you feel more comfortable keeping the wool over your eyes.

Now before I give you the signs I must take care to note that even though a great majority of these cult behaviors are practiced by the Jehovah's Witnesses NOT ALL of these behaviors are practiced by them. I also want to note that these are behaviors practiced by any cult, religious or non-religious, mainstream or not.

Signs that you belong to a cult are: the group displays excessively zealous and unquestioning commitment to its leader regarding its belief system or practices as Truth or Law.

- Questioning, doubt or dissent are discouraged or even punished; Mind altering practices (such as meditation *familiar practice to Witnesses*, chanting, speaking in tongues, denunciation sessions and debilitating work routines) are used in excess and serve to suppress doubts about the groups or its leaders.

- The leadership dictates, sometimes in great detail, how members should think, act and feel (for example, members must get permission to date, change jobs, marry- or leaders prescribe what type of clothes to wear, where to live, whether or not to have children, how to discipline children and so forth).

- The group is elitist, claiming a special exalted status for itself, it's leader(s) and members (for example the leader is considered the Messiah, a special being, an avatar-or the group and/or the leader is on a special mission to save humanity).

- The group has a polarized us-verses-them mentality, which may cause conflict with the wider society.

- The leader is not accountable to any authorities (unlike,

for example, teachers, military commanders or ministers, priests, monks and rabbis of mainstream religious denominations).

- The group teaches or implies that its supposedly exalted ends justify whatever means it deems necessary. This may result in members participating in behaviors or activities that would have been considered reprehensible or unethical before joining the group (for example, lying to family and friends, or collecting money for bogus charities).

- The leader induces feelings of shame and/or guilt in order to influence and/or control members. Often, this is done through peer pressure or sudden forms of persuasion.

- Subservience to the leader or groups requires members to cut ties with family and friends, and radically alter the personal goals and activities they had before joining the group.

- The group is preoccupied with bringing in new members.

- The group is preoccupied with making money.

- Members are encouraged or required to live and/or socialize only with other group members.

- The most loyal members (the "true believers") feel there can be no life outside the context of the group. They believe there is no other way to be, and often fear reprisals to themselves or others if they leave (or even consider leaving) the group. -source (Characteristics Associated with Cultic Groups by Janja Lalich, Ph.D. & Michael D. Langone Ph.D.; www.icsahome.com)

Any sources description of a cult will be pretty much the same as the source I referred to, as noted above. Personal research and knowledge of the organization should always be sought before joining and even before exiting. This holds true for any religious affiliation.

A mind without knowledge is the worst kind of incarceration. That's a motto I came up with so that I may never cease educating myself every single day.

Chapter 16

Appreciation for the Freedom of Choice

From all of the foretold and failed prophecies to the overwhelming amount of conditional love, my research told me that for more than just emotional reasons that it was time to leave this organization. Being mentally tortured for the sake of false religion was no longer acceptable.

From learning just how lucrative the Watchtower really is from donations made by members worldwide for each and every piece of literature published and for every meeting attended around the world, to understanding why they discontinued charging for the literature and instead began accepting donation to receive tax breaks and not to benefit the public, to reading a letter of their direct involvement with the United Nations (UN) whom they claim will attempt but will fail to be the very destruction of the Witnesses, the wild beast, I knew there was no turning point. There was no reasoning. I was finally able to see the point of this religion.

Their involvement with the UN was a big shock to me. Their affiliation with the Department of Public Information (DPI) of the UN as a Non-Governmental Organization (NGO) was from 1992 to 2001. They were formally disassociated from the UN as of March 4, 2004. Why would they have any affiliation at all with the wild beast?

The emotions began to come back so suddenly as I knew that I had made up my mind but that my choice to leave could cost me everyone who actually seemed sincere - which weren't very many. But most of all it could cost me my mother and my very own child who chose to take the religion as seriously as I had taught her to. She was quickly approaching legal adulthood so I allowed her to "choose." That is something I never had the freedom to do. I did draw a line though. If she crossed this line as far as her attitude towards me for being an ex-Witness - if that line was crossed or expectations were not met then I would not allow her to go to any more meetings or associate with anymore Witnesses until she was eighteen years old. Fortunately this was never an issue.

I did know one thing. My other children would never step another foot inside another kingdom hall ever again. I also knew that I had a responsibility to educate my children and allow them to educate themselves enough to make their own informed decisions as adults. At that point it would be my responsibility to allow them to "choose" their own religious path as long as no one gets harmed in the process. I will continue to support and love my children always.

Chapter 17

My Emotional Journey into Freedom

(Appreciation for Life Instilled)

This part of my journey was filled with much emotion and a greater awareness and appreciation for life as we know it. This is when I began to realize that religion in general was a hindrance in the search for true appreciation for life. To truly be happy meant that I would have to cease all expectations of gaining a prize of eternal life that I would never be worthy of it, nor was it promised to me or anyone else. I just wanted to appreciate life as I knew it. Live in the here and now. Smell the flowers. Admire the trees and sing along with the birds.

It is my opinion that religion restricts people from true appreciation because every single part of life has a condition. Love is under the condition that you agree with and live by their doctrines. Ironically they teach that love for God is conditional without even realizing it. Anytime a person puts their blood, sweat and tears into trying to please God so they may gain a prize of eternal life on earth or in heaven, they are worshipping selfishly. With all the horrible things we see and experience in daily living, I'd like to see how many faithful worshippers of God there would be if there was no reward attached.

Our children are supposed to love us even if we don't have a lot of money or material things. They should love us and appreciate us for the things that we can and do provide for them no matter how seemingly small it appears. Hard times should bring the children closer to their parents. This is unconditional love. There are no promises of anything grand attached. Love doesn't need to be purchased or bribed. You can't possibly love our creator, our universe, if you expect to get something for everything that you give. Our love for life is what God wants. Yes I am capitalizing the "G" in God because now I am speaking in terms of spirituality and not religiously.

God doesn't require anything from us to ensure His happiness. Who are we? Our job is to live life and enjoy what we can. I have no idea why we suffer so much. No one knows. There is no scripture in the bible that can rationalize anything that goes on in this life. Love does NOT allow babies and life in general to suffer endless unfathomable torture because of the sins of two people. Two people "they say" existed but no modern man has ever known. Love does NOT expect faith to lay in the hopes of something or someone totally unseen with your life as collateral in case your faith ceases. But I do know that we didn't just get here just because.

We don't exist to perform some basic function such as the flowers and trees. They don't wonder what the purpose of life is as a tree or a flower. They don't even live by any set of rules. But their existence, unbeknownst to them, does serve a purpose. Humans, on the other hand, have the capacity to care about the purpose of anything. There is definitely a point to our creation. That point as far as we are concerned is to enjoy life NOW. We have no knowledge of nor any control over the rest. As long as we have the ability to show love and understand the positive effects that it has on life, this should be our purpose in life.

I began to view things about my father differently about this time. The man who made me feel unwanted if not unloved, the man who appeared absent more than present and the man who I was taught to shun and ultimately damn to destruction would prove to be the flashlight that gave me the vision that I needed to see through my journey to freedom.

His stories that were never shared with me were finally shared. His fears, regrets and decisions were disclosed to me, but now my mind was free of judgment. I began to see him as a real human being with real feelings and now even though I still feel that he may be disappointed in me for not achieving a certain level of financial success I don't take it personally anymore because I now view myself as a real human being and not some robot damned to an existence of eternal judgment. The only issue I have is maybe why he didn't try a little harder to warn us about the organization. I know better, yet the child in me, wishes he would have demanded all the way to court that we leave this religion. To some this may seem a bit extreme but the mental damage I experience today, although to a much milder degree, is very real.

Chapter 18

My Mother's Humorous Yet Offensive Reaction

I was a nervous wreck drafting my exit letter and then drafting a second letter just to tell my mother, who slept downstairs from me, that I was leaving the organization. It would be not my mother's expected reaction but the shocking and unexpected reaction of the elders that would not only shock me but that would confirm my decision to leave. What's funny is that I never intended to tell the elders. I was simply going to fade away because I was so done answering to them. Of course my mother would be the one who would insist on calling them to come over, hence my letter to them as well after giving my mother her notice.

First, I said a prayer to guide me to the correct words to explain why I am leaving. I did not want to say I'm leaving because I don't believe the things they say or because I have a problem with the people. I wanted them to know that I had done my homework. I wanted to give them something to go home and think about and talk about.

But before I would write my formal disassociation letter to the Watchtower, I would write to my mother. She is the only person that I was straight and to the point with. Explaining anything to her no matter what evidence you presented to her would get you labeled an "apostate," which, by the way, only means a person who abandoned or left a former religion or belief. So actually that would make her and probably most Witnesses an apostate because she left a former religion to become a Jehovah's Witness.

My mother would, of course, ask me why I am leaving Jehovah. She looked at me as if her breath were literally being taken away from her. She had heard the worst news in her life. I was exceptionally close to her so for me to walk away from the only thing that seemed to keep her alive, was indeed a blow to her. Watching her reaction made me nervous. I was even somewhat saddened but I was prepared to lose her because for once in my life I had felt almost 100% positive that my decision was the correct one and for me that was enough. I accepted that anyone who would abandon me was simply ignorant - nothing personal.

My mother then started asking me in a completely different and almost sarcastic tone who I had spoken to that convinced me to leave. This question was followed by her placing her hands onto her hips and releasing a lopsided smirk as she shook her head at me. I no longer felt like her daughter but like a distant former Witness relative whom she had just chalked up as being officially "CRAZY." My sadness and nervousness would soon turn into anger because I was being completely disrespected as if I had committed any sin at all by leaving. So she informed me that she is required to tell the elders and that I am required to speak to them about my choice to leave.

Still not officially an ex-Witness, well, as least not on paper, I still had a lot of things to let go of and to come to a realization of. So telling the elders would be something that I didn't feel that I should have to do but I wasn't exactly ready to debate about it. So I proceeded up the stairs and into my room so that I could type and print my exit letter to the Watchtower. My plan was to give a VERY detailed letter to the elders for their reading enlightenment before they forwarded a copy to the Watchtower for the records and just say "adios." It turned out a bit more different than planned.

Chapter 19

The Elders' Reaction
Was My Confirmation

The elders wasted very little time making their way over to my house. When I stepped outside I knew that I had to keep this short. These elders were the ones that I spoke to often. Their wives were close to my mother and my daughter. They appeared shocked and slightly hesitant to approach me. We said our hellos and then I placed the letter into the hands of one. He immediately gathered the nerve to ask me what exactly had happened to cause me to come to my decision. I told him it was all in the letter.

He seemed eager at this point and pulled out his bible as the others followed his lead. I told them to close their bibles because I've read it enough to know the meaning of any scripture they were planning to show me and that it wouldn't help. As they closed their bibles, completely shocked, I felt a sudden sense of power. I just told some elders to close their bibles and without question or debate they listened. Is this what freedom from the Watchtower would bring? Did they actually just do as I told them to do without incident? My goodness this was a special feeling of liberation for me!

I felt a lot more confident at this point so I shared a bit of the information that I had researched and found to be true. I told them about the holidays that were celebrated and when they ended. I told them of the organization's former UN involvement. I went into great detail about these things.

The conversation outside of my home lasted about a half an hour. At this point it became silent very briefly followed by one of the elders asking who or what the source of my information was. I told him many reliable sources. He then asked if my sources were apostates. I asked him to tell me what an apostate is. He looked confused and I intervened. I told him the dictionary's definition for apostate and that this was also mentioned in my letter.

The shocking part happened at this point when one of the more silent elders suddenly said to me, "You know something? You are very smart." That statement was followed quickly by another elder agreeing that I am indeed very smart. I thought to myself, now wait a minute. I just blasted the organization to their faces and they in turn tell me how smart I am?

That let me know immediately that, not only did they know that what I had told them was true but they were shocked that a member of the rank and file would actually know all of this hidden inside information. Actually, this information was not so hidden but just widely ignored because no one ever looked outside of the organization for information.

I felt happy at this point. So the elders warned me that they would have to treat me like an apostate and was I ready for this? My reply was that I had already been treated as an outcast by the members of this religion since childhood and that it made no difference now. I told them that I wasn't disassociating myself from the people but I was disassociating myself from the religion and the organization. I let them know that if they stopped speaking to me that it would be on their own terms and not mine. The elders simply said ok. Then one by one I received what would be the only true loving brotherly hug I would ever receive from any elder, ever. They gave me a big and meaningful hug and walked away.

Their reaction spoke volumes to me. I often wonder just how many people are there for reasons not related to faith in or love for the religion. How many of those elders wanted out so badly but held on for the sake of fear or power or uncertainty in any other way. I wondered how many faithful servants knew that something was wrong but they were literally afraid to even entertain the thought of looking into their concerns. Then there are some who honestly are so blinded that they don't even care what's wrong, they just want some belief. Life without belief in something that gives life a direct purpose is too uncomfortable for far too many people. They would rather live a lie than face any possibility of faith shattering truth.

One of the elders offered me a ride to help with moving my mother's belongings into her new place as she was advised to do. He spoke to me now more intimately than he ever did when I was attending the Kingdom Hall. He told me about his life before becoming a Witness.

At the end of the ride back to my home he told me with sincerity and genuine love that if I ever needed anything that I could always call him. If he wasn't in the door to door ministry and was otherwise able to, he would assist me. It almost seemed like my exit from the religion made them more comfortable, or at least this particular elder, more comfortable with being himself and not an "elder" of a congregation.

Chapter 20

Life 101

(Introduction to Normal Human Life)

Suddenly I realized there was this thing called "Life." It didn't come with so many rules and stipulations. On Saturday mornings I did not have to choose between going to the doors of strangers to save our lives or staying in bed and enjoying life. People didn't appear wicked to me anymore.

What I did find was that I was sort of alone in a new world. I had to start from the beginning and navigate my way through the world without the direction of men dictating my every step. It was scary and equally exciting. I was given freedom and I had to figure out what to do with all of this newly found freedom - but - I learned a valuable set of lessons.

Before you damn someone to judgment even in your own mind, always consider their side of the story. People are not as evil as religion makes them out to be. "Love" is law. Everything else is worthless without love.

Spirituality brings greater appreciation for the things around you more than any amount of religion. If you're going to worship whoever you deem God to be, do it in spirit and in truth. Spirit comes from within. It is defined by your own heart condition. It creates oneness with peace that no man made entity could ever achieve. Spirituality makes a person more aware of their own strengths as well as weaknesses so a person is more likely to work on their flaws because they are working from a sincere force within themselves - their spirit.

We are all just trying to figure everything out. Some have tougher battles than others but inside we are all fragile beings just trying to figure everything out from our next move in life to surviving everyday life. Love does not condone obvious evils. Love unifies goodness from all sources and this is what life is about. "Love shuns all evil and unifies all goodness." This is a quote from my own heart and mind.

Chapter 21

From the Outside Looking In

One of my cousins blocked me from his Facebook page and stopped sending me emails of the next Watchtower lessons and information on anxiety and panic attacks as he suffers the same. He is an elder in another state. When I had told him that I was no longer a Witness it was annoying to see how quickly he deleted me from his life, yet he still spoke to non-Witness family members simply because they were either never baptized or they just faded out which meant that they were not technically disfellowshipped. How stupid is that! He also boasts of his personal friendship with a well known entertainer who is also a Jehovah's Witness, George Benson.

Although we are admonished not to be doing the things of the world or in association with people of the world, there are double standards as I mentioned early. Recall to the mind Prince, Venus and Serena Williams, Katherine Jackson, just to name a few. They have a different set of rules and expectations for serving God's only true spirit directed organization.

When I see the average religious person from almost any religion and especially Christianity, I see a bunch of uptight, overly eager and anxious people just waiting for the next wave of major news events to be followed by the coming of Christ or Armageddon. They can never see anything for what it is. Just another war! Just another disease! Just another murder! Just another terrorist attack!

Since 1914 the Witnesses have warned that we are living in the last days and that the signs of the last days would be food shortages, pestilence, earthquakes occurring in one place after the other, no natural affection, lovers of money rather than lovers of god, lovers of pleasure rather than lovers of people and goodness. Well, my question is: "have they ever read the Old Testament?"

There seemed to be war going on at every turn. People were worshipping a Golden Calf instead of God. There were harlots all over the place. Does Jezebel ring a familiar bell? Nothing is new under the sun. The only thing that has changed is the date. In fact as horrible and terrifying and even sometimes as downright depressing as life can be today, it seems like a great improvement since biblical times - even since modern day history. Yet people eagerly anticipate a dark cloud with Christ coming to destroy the evil and to save them as life continues to pass them by. I'm not trying to be funny I really think it's sad.

For the Witnesses who anticipate the coming destruction of this system of things, they rarely refer to the bible. How ironic! ALL information comes from all of the literature that the Watchtower prints up which, of course, is written by imperfect men. The bible however is just a supplement to the literature that they print and distribute. When a person studies they study out of books and magazines that only refer to the bible for scriptures cherry picked by the Watchtower to force feed whatever they want the bible study students and the members to believe.

I wonder if anyone has ever taken the time to actually think about that. How can a student effectively learn the meaning of the bible by reading and studying every Watchtower book available from cover to cover and the bible is used only sporadically? Of course the bible in itself is questionable to an extremely large degree but the issue here is that the bible is claimed to be God's words directly so why not use God's words directly and study with people reading THIS book from cover to cover no matter how long it takes? I wonder how many people, if any, actually took the time to think about this.

Understanding that this would be questionable to the average thinking human being, one has to also question why so many book are published and REQUIRED to be used by all members and placed in the door to door ministry. Think about it. If this religion operates worldwide and is very much united, and every single book published is done so on a worldwide basis at the same times for each and every convention held each year (in 2014 alone there were 193 International conventions in 71 cities worldwide; this figure for 2014 does not include the summer district conventions held worldwide over a period of two to three month and the circuit conventions usually held worldwide about four times each year) AND money is put into contribution boxes for every congregation worldwide who meet two to three times weekly and there are presently almost 8 million active witnesses worldwide, how much money are these people getting?

Do the math. This is a billion dollar publishing company. What makes it so much more lucrative over other religions that require or ask for donations is their unity? They are very united and bloody organized.

They say that their united and organized way of operating is another sign that they are the only religion of the true God because God is a God of organization. Actually it's great business practice though unfortunately dishonest and misleading. It is imperative that they keep and gain as many members as possible in order to keep this sort of money flowing in. The minute that people catch on to their agenda and false doctrine, their business becomes threatened. Remember - the word spreads fast! And so does the truth when people find it and expose it.

No one who relies on religion to find purpose can truly find happiness. This is because they are now spending every waking moment trying to be as close to perfect so that they won't go to hell or in order that they may not forever perish in Armageddon. Some people look forward to the hope of being reunited with their dead loved ones. I completely understand that feeling. But freedom and dictatorship can never be compatible. You can't have freedom in prison. You can't have freedom when other entities are required to think for you. You CHOOSE freedom when you let go of the fear of consequence that religion brings. Fear stifles most people from progressing. Letting go of this fear is when freedom becomes an option. Too many people are afraid to choose freedom out of fear and this is disheartening.

Chapter 22

Finding My Father in Spirit and Truth

Thinking back to my father who was once a faithful witness as he was born into this religion, I do not condone any of his actions that hurt my mother and dismantled our family but I do have more insight as to how a good person can make selfish decisions. As it was told to me he started associating with people of different cultures who studied different religions and philosophies.

My guess is that someone said something that caused great conflict between him and his Jehovah's Witness trained conscience. He probably felt that inner struggle that caused him to react instead of to think. One thing that I do know is that he could not have been at peace before he was disfellowshipped after he became inactive in the religion. People react differently to conflict.

I now understand that I may never fully understand my father's actions or words and that it's ok not to understand. I am happy that I no longer view any of his actions as something personal against me. And even if he had something personal against me it still wouldn't matter to me at this point because I did something so awesome that nothing can take that joy from me. I left that religion. Yes, it is that deep.

I love my father. I miss him dearly. I don't see him nearly enough but when I do I inwardly regress into a childlike state of mind. I dread knowing that the visit will end and that my father will go home. I never told him but his thirst for knowledge and education has rubbed off on me deeply. It is my freedom from the religion that made me discover how much we are alike in this regard.

Now that I can think for myself and learn whatever I want I accumulate knowledge of everything and I instill this into my children I just try not to be critical. I refuse to let anyone take my mind and my right to use it. No one is ever allowed to have that sort of control over me or my children ever again.

I am more aware of the conflicts of others around me and how it affects them, not because they are bad but because they are human. Even though I realize this is the true way to view people and life there is still a sort of hesitation inside of me when I think about calling my dad. It's not because I think he is a bad person or that he doesn't love me anymore, it's a learned behavior.

I learned that love was conditional. I have come a long way since my exit but some things I must still unlearn because they were so deeply ingrained in my mind and heart. I guess I have to learn that whatever I feel I may not have become in my father's eyes or whatever I may not have measured up to in his eyes has no bearing on his love for me. Though it's hard to separate these feelings of condition in my mind I know that it is essential and I am closer to achieving the "unlearn" status each day.

Chapter 23

Words of Encouragement

This is for those with questions and/or doubts. We were all born with common sense even if we push the "opt out" icon for using it. It's still there for our convenience if we should find that we need it. The best part is that no matter how hard someone may try or how much power someone may appear to have, your common sense is something that no one can take from you.

Universally most experiences from ex-Jehovah's Witnesses are extremely identical. If you were to put your fear of independent thinking aside for just one moment and actually read some of these reviews or talk to some of these ex-Jehovah's Witnesses about their reasons for leaving you will find that at least ninety percent of the people universally had the same questions and doubts about the organization.

Members of the organization, well-meaning and otherwise, will tell you that Satan is influencing you and that, in fact, it is YOU who you need to examine. We all are familiar with the drill. As much as independent thinking is frowned upon I think deep down that every single member realizes that there is something very fundamentally wrong with this restriction. If you are discouraged from thinking for yourself then you are being controlled. That's common sense.

No matter what anyone says to stifle you there is no hiding from the fact that everyone around the world has the same questions, doubts and experiences. Common sense tells you that this is no coincidence. Common sense tells you that the questions and doubts that you have does matter and it is important because chances are everyone else has or had those same doubts and questions. No matter how much you try to ignore your doubts common sense won't let you.

Do you want to be mentally incarcerated or do you want to be free? I was afraid just like you. I was probably brainwashed more than you. I was told I would die. I was and I still am called an apostate as if that word is another name for Satan. I was told all of these things, yet here I am living and feeling freedom that you won't experience stuck in the dependent thinking position.

The universe is not going to conveniently agree on all matters as the Watchtower tries to enforce upon its members universally. That is the beauty of life, well - most of the time. The one thing however, that is non debatable and pretty much universally agreed upon is love. When someone tells you that you must not love good people because they do not worship in the same manner as you do, it is time to start thinking for yourself. That mentality does affect you directly.

Chapter 24

Your Questions are Justified and You Positively Will Not Die for Thinking

Take a look at life. Take a look at everything around us. We should reasonably expect that any message from God should be given to us in a way that we can understand as imperfect humans. When we read in the bible that if we ask then we shall receive, there should be no other way to interpret that. That statement sounds pretty cut and dry to me. When we read in the bible that if we ask for anything according to God's will we shall receive, again it should mean exactly what it says.

I don't care how much faith you have there is no way that you can honestly ignore the fact that when people pray to God for babies to heal, sometimes, those babies not only die but they suffer along the way. For the Jehovah's Witnesses who say that Jehovah takes care of his faithful servants, please tell me why a loving and unbiased elder was shot to death while providing for his family? Why have I ever attended a funeral of a Jehovah's Witness? If a parent asks God to protect their children and then their child gets raped and/or murdered, tell me how in the world does this equate to unquestionable faith in an entity that we cannot see or hear? Surely these prayers would be in harmony with God's will.

Let's talk about faith. Do you really have faith as you sit and accept everything that is told to you and you only research in ways that you are told or allowed? How can you say that you have faith that you will live forever but yet you visit doctors and take medicine for your health and survival? If I have faith that my husband is faithful, I'm not going to put a GPS tracking device on his car and phone just to be certain that he is being faithful. Faith means that you believe in something that you cannot prove and it is not testable. You just believe based upon something that someone told about this person or thing. Faith is not absolute. It is not the truth.

What's sad is that you will not die for asking justifiable questions. You will not die for wondering or for seeking answers. You are using your brain. You are refusing to behave as a robot and you are behaving as a normal human being. If your mate cheats on you do you sit there and say, "Well they must have had a reason for doing it and since I have faith in their love for me I will not question them?" No. You would question them and you would not be satisfied until they gave you satisfactory answers. If they continue to cheat most likely you will assume that they don't really value the union, so you would leave. Well, I'm not saying to leave God, I'm saying you should ask questions because bad things keep happening over and over and yet people have faith that people are supposed to be tortured for some higher purpose. You cannot possibly believe this.

There is nothing that my children can possibly do that would make me allow them to suffer and even though it's within my power to stop it, I choose not to. That is not logical. My children should not be expected to understand that and I should not expect them to understand that. If my eldest child robbed a store why am I going to cause my other children to suffer and even allow them to die because of the sin of my eldest child? That is cruel. That is insane. Furthermore if badness was wiped out with the Flood and again in Sodom and Gomorrah, what has it accomplished? Why do we still sin and why are we still paying for the mistakes of two people that we will never know? How can the most faithful individual not question these things?

The purpose of this particular part of the book is to encourage people to stop being robots. You cannot remain oblivious to the fact that nothing much makes any sense. If you have questions, concerns, doubts, etc…talk about it. Ask about it. You should research the things you are willing to die for. You should expect to have your prayers answered if you have faith in the bible. You should expect to be shielded from crime if this is what you believe in the name of Jesus or Jehovah or Allah or Yaweh or Jah or whomever your undying and unquestionable faith lays with. If you find that any of the things promised to you are not happening for most of or for all of your life, you need to ask questions, especially if your life depends upon it.

Chapter 25

My Random Thoughts and Current Beliefs

I do believe in God. I don't believe we just came about from some matter or any other way except creation. I personally don't question God's existence, I question God. I want to know why an all loving Being watches us die in gruesome ways every day. I want to know why an all-powerful Being would refuse to use this power to stop evil from happening to good people. The biggest issue I have is why a "perfect" Being would create evil in the first place? How can evil come from an all perfect loving Being?

I'm certainly not claiming to be correct nor am I trying to be correct. I'm simply exploring what I feel are logical ideas. My first thought is that God is a loving God. I believe he is in fact all loving. My second thought is that God is powerful but not all powerful. I believe that God is fallible. That would answer all of my questions concerning the past and the present. That would help me to understand why God tried to create us as perfect as possible when he caused the flood and again when he destroyed Sodom and Gomorrah. He was striving for something that he was not able to achieve.

I believe we are made in God's image. For this reason I also believe that God gets angry and jealous like we do. I believe God cries when we suffer because he can't take our pain away. Since I feel God is more humane than we have always been taught to believe, I feel closer to God and I love him more because I can personalize him now.

Again, I'm not seeking to be correct. This is the only logical explanation that I can think of. If we are able to feel love then our Creator is able to feel love. If we are able to feel any of the emotions that we feel then our Creator is able to feel the same. My honest belief is that none of us will ever know the truth. We try to replace our current thoughts with proof of other things and the truth is that we can't. This does not mean the questions should stop. Questions help you to seek God in an unrestricted manner.

Hopefully your search for truth will bring you to become more appreciative and more aware of humanity. I no longer look down on Atheists because they actually have some informative things to say. They are in the same boat, unknowing. Not believing in God is what seems the most logical to them. My thoughts are no better or correct than theirs.

Never stop seeking. You may not find the answer you are looking for or you may find the answer you are looking for. I promise though that the journey that comes with learning and broadening our minds is amazing. You appreciate different cultures and different ways of living. You learn tolerance and indifference. You also learn that no one is any better than the next person. Most of all it teaches you to love. It certainly taught me to love because it taught me indifference and tolerance. I will forever embrace my freedom of thinking and of choice.

Chapter 26

Freedom from Religion Does Not Equal Freedom to Misbehave

Freedom from religion does not give us the right to behave immorally or unethically. Religion should not be the fabric that holds a person's morale together, your heart should be. This is the importance of living, learning and loving in Spirit and Truth.

Don't allow new found freedom to relieve you of your duties to be a good person. Don't allow your standards to fall because you no longer have the chains of religious oppression holding you hostage. If you weren't an alcoholic before, don't join the crowd later. If you weren't promiscuous before, don't become that way later.

I truly hope that my words and my experiences may serve as an eye opener. I'm not looking for confirmation. I am not concerned with who may not agree with me. I hope that weather you agree or not you still received an eye opening lesson somewhere in my story. Most of all, if my story and my words of encouragement guides only one person into their journey to freedom, my mission is accomplished and I will sleep well.

I respect everyone's beliefs as long as it does not involve conditional love, mind control, discouragement from asking questions, repression of concerns or independent thinking and research, judging, shunning, not respecting the beliefs of others, condemning others to hell or claiming to be the only way.

I love you all and may you find the true meaning of unconditional love and practicing that love in Spirit and in Truth. May you seek and keep a very personal relationship with whoever you believe your higher power to be. Just be sure that love is always in the equation. Never allow anyone to take your freedom and your right to think away from you. When you understand that true freedom in this world comes without stipulations and always with love, you will then understand the true meaning of freedom.

One Love!

Epilogue

Today many, who are interested in becoming a Jehovah's Witness, will see a slight contrast in the way the organization is ran today and the things that I experienced as an active witness. The vast majority of the things mentioned about how the religion operates, its organization, as well as the rules that it enforces upon its members still apply today. However, there have also been huge changes made in the organization that would have not only been discouraged but also forbidden in prior years. These changes actually appear to blend them in closely with other organizations so they actually appear to be more of a mainstream religion, yet they still believe and preach that they are God's only true spirit directed organization and that being a Jehovah's Witness is the only way to worship the true God. They fail to realize that having many pages on Facebook to witness to others, having a new online broadcasting program, having a Jehovah's Witness dating site, and other radical changes, is actually counterproductive to their claims that being different is a sign that they are the true religion. It goes to prove that this organization is still changing what is acceptable and is the truth.

Just remember these few words that my father recently told me: "Truth Never Changes!"

(I'd like to note that my mother chose to love me instead of shunning me. My daughter chose to love me and clings to me even more as a young adult. We have a very strong mother and daughter bond. My mother and I also still maintain a very strong mother and daughter bond and aside from the reminders I still get about the so called "truth," my mother and I still maintain a strong inseparable bond.)

About the Author

Ritchie Mac brings to the fore the controversial matters that many shy away from. She addresses issues that are not necessarily main stream but they are the true life experiences that affect our societies as a whole. She also addresses other non-fictional issues in an effort to bring people together so that we may learn to address our experiences, embrace our differences, debate peaceably, and agree that love should be our common denominator no matter what.

HOLY

TERROR

In The Name of

The Father

The Son and

The Watchtower

Ritchie Mac

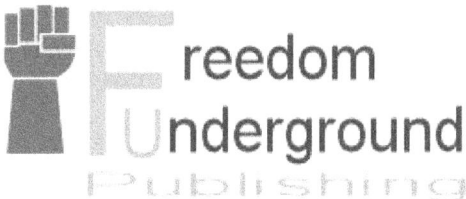

www.ingramcontent.com/pod-product-compliance
Lightning Source LLC
LaVergne TN
LVHW021402080426
835508LV00020B/2419